THE REFERRAL RULES!

7 WAYS TO GET MORE PROFITABLE REFERRALS

TIMOTHY M. HOUSTON

WWW.TMHOUSTON.COM

Houston-CB Group, Inc., publisher

Copyright © 2015, by Timothy M. Houston.

All rights reserved.

All trademarks or registered trademarks, logos and brand names and trade names used and referenced herein are property of their respective owners.

No part of this publication may be reproduced, stored in a retrieval system, or transmitted by any means, electronic, mechanical, photocopying, recording, scanning, or otherwise, except as permitted by Section 107 or 108 of the 1976 United States Copyright Act without the prior written permission of the copyright owner. Requests for permission or further information should be addressed to: Houston-CB, Group, Inc.at requests@tmhouston.com.

ISBN-13: 978-1522813811

This publication contains the opinions and ideas of its author. It is intended to provide helpful and informative material on the subjects addressed. While the author and publisher have used their best efforts in preparing this book, the strategies outlined herein may not be suitable for every individual and are not guaranteed or warranted to produce any particular results. This publication is designed to provide accurate and authoritative information in regard to the subject matter covered. It is sold with the understanding that the author and publisher are not engaged in rendering legal, financial, accounting, or other professional services. The reader should consult with a competent professional before adopting any of the suggestions in this book or drawing any inferences from it.

No warranty is made with respect to the accuracy or completeness of the information referenced or contained herein and both the author and publisher specifically disclaim any implied warranties of merchantability or fitness for a particular purpose and further disclaims any responsibility for any liability, loss or risk, personal or otherwise, which is incurred as a consequence, directly or indirectly, of the use and application of any of the contents of this book. Neither the author nor publisher shall be held liable for loss of profit or any other commercial damages, including but not limited to special, incidental, consequential or other damages.

Dedicated to the memory of my father, Timothy E. Houston

Table of Contents

REFERRALS ARE NOT AN ENTITLEMENT! 1

WHAT ARE THE REFERRAL RULES? 11

RULE #1: DEVELOP REFERRAL ENABLERS 14

RULE #2: IT IS ALL ABOUT THE EXPERIENCE. 20

RULE #3: REFERRAL RICHES ARE IN NICHES .. 25

RULE # 4: BREAK IT DOWN TO BUILD IT UP ... 33

RULE #5: RECONNECT TO GET REFERRED 37

RULE #6: FOLLOW UP OR FALL OUT 54

RULE #7: GIVE THANKS…AND FEEDBACK 60

BEFORE YOU GO 64

MEET TIM HOUSTON 66

ENDNOTES 68

REFERRALS ARE NOT AN ENTITLEMENT!

I attend hundreds of business networking meetings and events within the course of a year; so it wasn't a surprise that on a beautiful summer evening I found myself traveling to yet another networking event in New York City.

After a while many of these events seem alike: you have great, productive networking groups like BNI that are focused on helping business people to generate referrals through a structured positive, professional, category-exclusive program. Then there are the events which serve as over-glorified mixers that most people attend just for the drinks and the food all the while trying to sell their products or services within ten seconds of meeting a new person.

But this particular networking event really made me curious when the invitation said that the host and his staff would act as "referral concierges" throughout the event to every attendee and which included the bold claim that attendees were "guaranteed" to walk out of the event with at least one referral.

When I arrived there were about 150 people swarming across the rooftop bar atop of one of the trendiest hotels in Manhattan. Some were admiring the breathtaking views as the sun started its slow decent over the western portion of the iconic New York City skyline while others were spending their time chatting at the bar with drinks and food in-hand. Others went around striking up conversations, giving and collecting business cards faster than a dealer at a Las Vegas casino would deal a round of black jack.

So far, it seemed just like other networking events that I had been to in the past with some of the types of people I chronicled in *The World's Worst Networker* and still others who were networking with a purpose – that is until Phil, the organizer of the event, stood up on a chair in the middle of the bar and with microphone in hand, addressed the crowd.

After thanking everyone for attending and introducing himself and the sponsors of the event, he said: "As you all know, networking is important to do because it can help you to grow your business. But this event is different. You see, unlike most networking groups and most of the other networking events you go to where you are on your own, I feel that because you paid money and dedicated your time to be here tonight, that you are entitled to at least to walk out of here with at least one referral. "

"My staff and I are your referral concierges tonight. Just come over to us and we will refer you to someone else at this event who could use your services or who you can partner with to offer your products or services to," said Phil.

"Did I just hear this guy correctly? Because we showed up, we're '*entitled*' to referrals?" I thought to myself, "What they're just doing is trying to play matchmaker with the people who are here tonight. In my opinion, these aren't referrals; they are at best lukewarm introductions, to people who barely know one another!"

As I watched some of the referral concierges try to match people up, Phil wandered over to me and asked what I did because he could probably refer me to someone else there. Wanting to see where this would lead, I kept my description as generic as possible by telling him I was a marketing consultant that worked with businesses of all sizes.

"Great! I have just the person for you to meet! He's over here…hey Eric, come here I want you to meet this guy who could help you get more clients," he exclaimed as he dragged me by the arm to meet Eric, a young 20-soemthing who was introduced as the "Chief Relationship Officer" of a tech company based in Brooklyn. Phil then excused himself as he had to "refer" more people to each other, leaving Eric and me to carry on the conversation alone.

I asked Eric what his company does and after getting a very convoluted answer involving everything from SEO to social media management, before I had a chance to ask any questions, Eric asked what I did.

I told him that I make business more productive, profitable and prosperous by helping them to design referral marketing and generation programs as well as teaching people how to network effectively.

He didn't seem to be that interested in my answer as he reached for his smartphone and began to respond to a text, and then said "excuse me" and wandered off to a corner. It was at that point I decided to leave.

A few days later, I received the following email from Eric:

"Hey Tim,

It was great meeting you the other night at the networking event. I really hate networking but since Phil guaranteed that I would walk out with at least one referral I couldn't pass up the opportunity. He was right when he said that you can help me. I checked out your website and also Googled you and found that some of your clients include (name of large pharmaceutical company) and (name of major international news organization) and that you are a bestselling author. On LinkedIn, I noticed that you know people at (name of large insurance company) and you're friends with (name of politician)."

"It would be amazing and beneficial if you would provide me with a referral to your contacts at these companies because we have an amazing service which…."

…and he went on and on for another three lines at how great his company is and how they can help these two particular clients of mine.

Then he wrote:

"When can we meet in person or maybe we could Skype so we can go over how my company can improve your social media marketing strategy and get your website to the first page of Google so that you can dominate your industry? When we do meet, we can talk about the other businesses that you could refer to us so that they could experience our services."

I thought to myself that Eric and Phil, the organizer of the event, were possibly ignorant about referral marketing and development, a tad bit arrogant and obviously suffering from entitlement syndrome.

After composing my reply three times which I highly edited, I responded:

"Hi Eric,

As my friend, bestselling author and speaker Susan RoAne wrote in her book, *The Secrets of Savvy Networking*:

'Too many people feel that under the 'guise of networking' they are to be given leads, referrals and information that they have not earned. We earn these [referrals] by establishing communication and rapport'"

"In case you don't recall, immediately after asking what I did you decided to text your friend and then excused yourself from the conversation and wandered off. Not cool at all. That kind of behavior just breeds disdain and contempt from others. I was disappointed that a 'Chief Relationship Officer' of a company did that."

"And contrary to Phil's philosophy, I believe that it is a privilege to give and to receive referrals, not a right and certainly not an entitlement just because we both showed up to an event."

I wish I could say that my experience with Phil and Eric was just an isolated incident, however, having worked with thousands of business people from around the world for more than 20 years, I often experienced a strange phenomenon: too often many of them neglected the very basic fundamentals of their businesses. The same thing happened when it came to getting referrals for their business. Many focused on everything but the basics and in the end, they didn't get as many quality, qualified referrals as they could have.

So many people attend networking events, seminars, business card exchanges, Meetups and spend exorbitant amounts of money in advertising to chase after new, potential clients and referrals.

Unfortunately, some of them learned the hard way that:

- Just because you went to the networking mixer doesn't entitle you to referrals…

- Just because you did a great job for a client doesn't mean they will refer you…

- Just because you have the greatest product or service in the world, doesn't mean referrals will come your way…

- Just because you joined a networking group doesn't mean that the people you meet will give your referrals right away…

- Just because you have hundreds, thousands, tens of thousands or millions of followers on Twitter, "likes" and friends on Facebook or connections on LinkedIn doesn't mean that someone will recommend you to someone else…

- Just because you're nice, friendly, professional, honest or (insert any other positive adjective) doesn't mean you're referable…

In order to get referrals, you must earn them over and over and over again by continuously serving others and by keeping their best interests in mind.

To do this you need to know and follow **The Referral Rules.**

WHAT ARE THE REFERRAL RULES?

The Referral Rules are seven basic principles we probably know and yet many people forget or choose to ignore. If you are looking for a book with a whole lot of fluff or some long, complicated theories and strategies, then this isn't the book for you. As you read through these pages, you may become surprised – perhaps even a little embarrassed -- to recognize that you have become complacent in certain areas.

Following them will give you exactly what you need to do to earn qualified referrals for your business, over and over again.

WHAT IS A QUALIFIED REFERRAL?

Not everyone defines a qualified referral the same way. For the purposes of this book, I define a qualified referral in two ways:

1) A qualified referral is the ***privilege of the opportunity*** given to you by someone else to potentially do business with someone who wants, needs or desires the products or services that you offer; or

2)) A qualified referral is the ***privilege of the opportunity*** given to you by someone else for an introduction to a person or organization which can be either a potential source of new clients for your business or which could add value to your business in some manner.

Dictionary.com defines the word "privilege" as: "[A] right, immunity, or benefit enjoyed only by a person beyond the advantages of most.[i]"

When it comes to referrals, as the recipient of one you are enjoying a certain benefit that your competitors and colleagues are not. This is because the Giver of the referral has had a history of some sort of success with you. They implicitly trust you enough to put their reputation on the line when referring another person or an organization that *they* have a relationship with, to you.

This book is designed to be a quick read and will offer strategies and solutions which are incredibly easy to implement. It is purposely designed to return your focus to the basics so that your referral marketing and generation efforts can be more productive, profitable and prosperous.

RULE #1:

DEVELOP REFERRAL ENABLERS

Most books and programs on referrals and networking talk about finding and developing sources. While sources are incredibly important and needed, once discovered they must be cultivated and developed in order to reap the benefits they can provide. I believe that instead of just finding sources you need to find and develop referral enablers.

Often the word "enabler" is viewed and understood by most people as something negative, such as someone who encourages or helps another to engage in self-destructive behavior. But the actual word "enable" means "to supply with the means, knowledge or opportunity; make able" or "to make feasible or possible.[ii]"

Creating strong, reliable relationships with these people can not only just result in more referrals, but also propel your business to stratospheric heights.

The three most common types of referral enablers are:

The Connector: These are people who find joy and appreciation of being able to play matchmaker between people. They love to network and interact with people and they tend to appear to "know everyone." Because of their social nature, most of the time, their tone and topics of their conversations are about the people involved, not their own ideas.

Connectors must believe and have confidence in you as they will often refer a prospect based upon the prospect's need for an expert or authority. The Connector needs to believe that you would be the "best fit."

In general, a Connector's network of people tends to be rather broad; however the majority of the people within those networks tend not to have large amounts of influence on other people.

The Key Influencer: I think the best description of this type of enabler comes from The

Word-of-Mouth Marketing Association which defines a Key Influencer as "[A] person or group of people who possess greater than average potential to influence due to attributes such as frequency of communication, personal persuasiveness or size of and centrality to a social network, among others.[iii]" They are the people who can provide access to clients, potential referral sources, decision makers and partners and can help to change those people's behaviors.

Unlike Connectors who typically have large social networks, Key Influencers have smaller but deeper networks of people that also have a profound impact to influence others. Typically, Influencers are often found in niches based on their areas of interest or expertise and can create a huge "buzz" about your services and products.

But be aware that Key Influencers often have their own agenda. In exchange for referring business to you, they may want something in return – not necessarily money but perhaps complimentary samples or trials of your services or products. Sometimes, it's just public recognition. If they really like your services/products, Key Influencers can also be turned into Advocates who continue to refer over time but more often than not, Key Influencers are short-term referral sources.

The Advocate: Advocates are raving fans who are usually your current or past customers/clients/patients. They love your product and services so much that they seemingly tell everyone about it and frequently will refer others to you – so long as they remain passionate about your services and products. Advocates can also be Influencers in certain communities and markets and are implicitly trusted by their family members, friends, and social media followers. Unlike Key Influencers they often do not require any form of compensation and A are awesome long-term referral sources.

As you design and build your networks and develop your referral generation strategy you need to assess who are the current people in your various networks that fall within these three common categories. Remember, a person who belongs to multiple networks can have the qualities of the Advocate in one network, Key Influencer or Connector in another or none at all, depending on their role(s) and relationships within those networks.

Once you have identified the people in the various roles, you then need to engage them accordingly. For example, you can reach out to Advocate and ask them for a testimonial (written and/or video) that you can use in your marketing materials. You can provide them with free samples or discounted services as a thank you for their loyalty. If they are saying great things about you or your products or services on Social Media, acknowledge them as much and as often as possible.

For the Connectors, attend the events they attend or put on. If a Connector is hosting an event, contact them in advance and offer to help them in any way you can. Also don't be afraid to ask them for introductions to other people that you want to meet who will be attending the same event.

For Key Influencers, do everything you can to make them look good to the followers in respective niches or perhaps in your field as well. Give them a testimonial as to how their expertise, services or products have helped you in the past. Don't be afraid to ask them for help or advice as they frequently are willing to give it.

RULE #2:

IT IS ALL ABOUT THE EXPERIENCE

In 2008, Business Week reported:

"Choice-fatigued consumers are not looking for another product that hasn't taken their true needs and desires into consideration. They are looking for companies in which to believe and give their allegiance. They are looking for experiences that cater to their deep-seated desires. This type of engagement requires much more than the latest technological breakthrough: It requires emotional engagement [iv]."

Every business is in the experience business, regardless of the nature or type of business. The experience I'm referring to is not just the actual "doing" of business. It is how the business gets done and the feelings and emotions felt along the way with each particular step.

Companies stage an experience when they engage customers in a personal, memorable way[v]. People notice how you respond and communicate with them. They evaluate how they were treated, how good or bad their interaction with you and your staff was; how their needs were or weren't met; the ease or difficulty involved in working with you and of course, their overall satisfaction when the job or work was completed.

In order to become referable to others, you must go well beyond your clients' positive experiences with you. In fact, while your clients' positive experiences can lead to additional referrals for your business, it's a fact that not every satisfied client will refer you potential new clients.[1]

---

[1] In ***Leads To Referrals***, I explain the reasons and provide the research data that shows why most satisfied clients ***don't refer*** potential new business on an ongoing basis and I also reveal the steps, strategies and techniques you can put in place to motivate and change their behavior.

There are two other groups of people with whom you need to have good experiences with: Referral Enablers and those people you meet through your networking efforts.

The experiences that Referral Enablers and the people within your various networks have with you also play a big role in determining if you have earned the privilege of receiving their referrals. For example, it is a huge mistake to immediately ask for referrals from people you just met. You have very little to no credibility at this point in the relationship. What is appropriate to do is to follow-up and to stay in contact with those you meet through networking and then to take steps to create a series of positive experience as you build and nurture these new relationships.

These experiences do not need to be epic in size; in fact, a series of small and positive experiences ranging from a simple thank-you note to sending them a birthday card, or providing them with information that they could use to help them in their business or in some aspect of their life can go a long way in helping them decide that they will refer to you.

Along the way, you build the trust, confidence, the credibility and also prove your expertise and authority in your profession by demonstrating your willingness to assist or help the people that they know and trust.

You also educate them as a) what is a qualified prospect and b) how to refer qualified prospects to you in the manner you want them referred. Do not assume that they will know this. For example, you may be a florist and are willing to have a couple who recently got engaged drop by your store and tell you that Brian Jameson told you to stop by in order to discuss some wedding arrangements. On the other hand, you may be a business attorney who helps people to set up new businesses and wants to first speak to a potential client on the telephone before meeting them and would like to have your referral source call them in advance in order to provide an introduction before the consultation.

As for your Referral Enablers, their experiences with you are paramount to setting the stage to provide you with referrals. Everything that you say and do creates an experience point to which they will refer in their mind that helps to convince them why they should take a risk of their reputation -- or perhaps even a financial risk -- by referring their family member, client, friend, neighbor or strategic partners to you.

These experience points make the difference between referring to you versus your competitors. It is your responsibility as the recipient of any referral to make the person giving you the referral feel good, comfortable, safe and secure and always appreciated.

RULE #3:

REFERRAL RICHES ARE IN NICHES

Most of us have heard the advice that we should narrow down our business to serve certain niches (i.e. a specific market segment, or a group of people, etc.) in order to increase our profitability and to grow our business. Niche markets do not exist naturally and are created through the identification of the needs, wants and desires that are not being addressed or are underserved by others in your field. The creation occurs when you develop and deliver products and services to serve and satisfy those markets.

I am an advocate of niche marketing so long as there are enough people or businesses within a certain niche that have the resources to purchase your products/services. The advantage of working with niches is that you can be become the known "expert" for your field that becomes so well known by everyone in the niche. You are seen as a trusted advisor and your business could become the de facto provider of the specific products/services you offer to all those within the niche, filled with repeat business and referrals.

Essentially, when you niche your business or segments of it, you become a "big fish in a small pond" instead of being a "small fish in a big pond." (From my own experience, being a "big fish in a small pond" can be incredibly fun and very lucrative).

TWO HIDDEN SOURCES OF NICHE REFERRALS:

Most business people tend to spend a lot of their time and energy in identifying the niche and then finding new people or businesses within their niches who they can work with. For the established business who has served a wide variety of clients when they make a decision to "niche down," they sometimes overlook a potential referral gold-mine:

1) the niche markets within their current clients and 2) the niche markets that their clients serve or belong to.

Regardless of what your product/service is, there are different segments or niches within your current client/customer/patient base. Your job is to a) identify the different niches within your client base, b) then select one to three (maximum) that you would like more referrals from and c) then encourage and entice your current clients and referral partners for more referrals or introductions to people who work in these particular niches.

For example: Sandra is an independent representative with a popular multilevel marketing skin care company. While women make up almost 100% of her clients and are independent reps within her in downline, she wanted to focus on those who had young children and were interested in making some extra money without taking on a traditional part-time job. Sandra contacted those of her Referral Enablers that had ties with children's groups, PTAs and sports teams and asked for introductions to the women who fit her target market. Over the next 12 months, she was able to recruit 18 new reps as part of her downline.

CASE STUDY:

Ted is one of my clients who owned an office supply company that has hundreds of clients which range from solo entrepreneurs and non-profit organizations to Fortune 500 companies. Every day, his company had to compete against the big "chain" office supply stores. His 20 member sales team did everything from cold-call to join referral and networking groups like BNI in order to increase their client base.

Ted realized that there was no way he could outspend his bigger competitors in advertising by going after "everyone" like they did; so he decided that he wanted to increase the number of niche clients, particularly non-profit organizations and wanted help in developing a referral generation strategy that would help accomplish that goal.

Here are the steps that we took to identify their most profitable niche areas and positioned the company to serve and become the de facto office supply company to those niches.

Step 1: Ted and his staff divided their current client base into market segments and then into smaller niche areas. Looking for certain "trends", they found that non-profits represented about 27% of their current client base. Some of their non-profit clients focus on raising funds for research for diseases like cancer and HIV/AIDS. Others provide services to people with other serious health issues, such as autism or multiple sclerosis, and still other of their non-profit clients focus on more social issues, such as homelessness, drug addiction, adoption of older kids and job training for at-risk youth.

Step 2: We worked to identify three types of niche non-profits they wanted to focus on. With some research, they decided that that they would target non-profit organizations that focus on social issues, specifically those that help people with drug addiction and those that provide job training for at-risk youths or formerly incarcerated people. They identified three specific non-profits in their region that were not their and also identified the decision makers in each of these non-profits.

Step 3: Ted and his staff trained his sales and marketing teams to ask for specific referrals to these types of non-profits from their current client base and from their referral partners. When communicating with their current clients (in person, through social media, via email, and in phone calls), Ted's sales people mention that they are looking for introductions to directors or people who work for these three specific non-profits or others like them.

At networking events, business expos and seminars, they mention that although they work with a diverse client base, they enjoy and excel at working work with non-profits and that they are looking to meet with the directors (by name) of the three non-profits they were specifically targeting during this time.

Although it may seem a bit counter-intuitive or counterproductive, the more specific they were, the easier they made it for the people in their networks to provide an introduction to that person or a person in a similar position at another company or organization.

Step 4: We then looked for certain Referral Enablers that Ted's company had relationships with and other centers of influence within these niches. We found a few Advocates and two Key Influencers who were seen as experts in their fields. In speaking with these Enablers, Ted was able to learn more about the fundraising events and industry conferences they attend. Through these Enablers, Ted was able to be introduced to Directors and board members other, similar non-profits and charitable organizations.

Step 5: Ted's company began to sponsor different events and exhibit at seminars, conferences and expos that his niche clients attended. By increasing his company's presence and visibility, they developed a name for themselves as being the office supply store that catered to and specialized in working with various non-profits. As a result, Ted's company began to get more referrals both within and outside of the non-profit world.

Ted tapped into and developed a market share over the next 20 months that his competition completely ignored. In doing so, he created a whole new legion of Advocates who were loyal to his company and truly found that referral riches were found in niches.

RULE # 4:

BREAK IT DOWN TO BUILD IT UP

Two of the common mistakes that business people make are a) they are too general when it comes to asking for referrals for their business and/or b) that they ask for too much by providing a litany of things that they do.

To get higher quality and more rapid referrals, the opposite is true: you must concentrate on helping others to identify referrals for one segment of your business and you must be incredibly specific as to the person or organization you want referred.

For example: Instead of a CPA asking for referrals of people looking to have their tax returns prepared and filed, they could narrow it down to specific types of clients that they would like to work with, such as federal, state or city workers. Narrowing it even further, they could ask for referrals of retired federal, state or city workers or those who are nearing retirement.

When you appeal to a particular segment of your business and describe the various target audiences within that segment, your referral enablers are more likely identify potential clients to refer to you. The more you tell them about exactly what you're looking for increases the chances of getting a qualified referral.

At this point, the difficulty some people have is making sure that others understand their referral request. To ensure that they do, you need to first tell them what kind of referrals you want by illustrating it with a brief story and then you ask your current and former clients, referral partners, friends and family and Referral Enablers to provide them.

Here's an example using an insurance agent:

THE TELL: "As an insurance agent, it is important for me to educate my clients and prospects about preparing for life's unexpected events."

THE STORY: "For example, I recently worked with a couple who opened their own business a year ago. It's a plumbing business and the wife runs the business and the husband does the technical work. Two months ago, he was involved in a car accident in which he fractured his arm and a leg and thus he can't work for at least another month. But because they had an excellent disability policy in place, he is receiving some financial relief to get through these tough times."

THE ASK: "Can you recommend and refer someone that you know who may own their own small business or who works for a small business such as a plumber or electrician, so I can show and help them to protect themselves from events such as this one?"

Remember, the actual referral request needs to be crystal clear and incredibly simple. People do not need to know all of the nuances or intricate details about your business: they need to know who or what to look for that could be a referral opportunity, as well as what to say, how to say it and how to deliver that referral to you.

When you break your business down, keeping it simple it will actually build up and generate more qualified, profitable referrals for your business.

RULE #5:

RECONNECT TO GET REFERRED

We all have people who were once a part of our lives but now we have lost touch: friends from high school or college, someone we grew up with, neighbors who moved away, teachers who taught us. Eventually, our paths in life move us in different directions.

In business, it's no different. We started out with certain clients, suppliers, vendors, co-workers and employees. As the business grew and evolved, we made changes along the way; we hired new people when others left, we started new relationships with suppliers, we hired new vendors to sell our products. There may also have been relationships that we didn't tend "well enough" -- and they left us!

In business, however, a financial impact will be felt if we stray too far from those who have been referral sources. Most business people tend to focus a large percentage of their networking efforts to obtain new referrals. What about those past clients who came by way of referral? What about past referral sources? We spend hundreds of hours each year and thousands of dollars chasing after new business when we can and should further cultivate those relationships we currently have and have had with people who are already part of our networks.

In an ideal world, we should be in frequent contact with such people, but there will be times when, for some reason, a former referral source may stop referring to us or ceases to be in our circle, and thus we stop referring to them. This loss of contact often isn't due to any negative experience. We all experience normal drift, and perhaps we or they were "out of sight" and thus "out of mind".

There is hope though.

We *can* renew relationships with people from the past.

Sometimes we may feel uncomfortable when we've been out of contact for a long period of time. What stops us? Do we pick up the phone? Send a text? What do we say?

Once we believe there is value to overcoming the awkwardness, we need a technique to help us renew the relationship.

One way is through what I have termed to be **Reintroduction Referrals.**

If it's been a while since you last met with someone and feel awkward to reach out to them, ask your current referral partners and even your customers if they know that person. Find out how strong of a relationship they have and if it's strong enough say that you would like a reintroduction. (Yes, actually say reintroduction). Then ask if they would be willing to reintroduce you.

If they question why you want to be reintroduced, be honest. Tell them that you had met the person before and were thinking about them recently and wanted to make contact to learn how you and they could possibly help each other. Since your referral partner/customer has a strong relationship with the person, ask if they could help you in making the reconnection.

We all may have found ourselves in a social situation, such as a party or networking mixer where the host or a friend of ours reintroduces us to someone that they know well and have introduced to us to before. It's very common to hear people reintroduce each other by say something like "you remember Andrew and Kelly, the owners of Delicious Delights Catering on Main Street."

But what if our referral partners do not have a direct contact with the person we want to become reacquainted with?

Here's another approach that could help you to start again.

Step 1: Do Your Research.

If it's been a long time (i.e. over a year) since you last communicated with the person, do some homework before contacting them. A simple search on Google could reveal some information that you can use as a way to open the door to a conversation. Social networking sites like Facebook could reveal life changes such as they got married or had a child. Sites like Linked In are also useful because you can see their networks and who may you know in common. This can serve as a foundation to further conversation and also allows you to easily reach out to those in your network to ask for a reintroduction.

Step 2: Get Their Attention!

In today's society, communicating is as easy as sending email, a text message, an instant message, a note or making a phone call. While the benefits to instant communication are numerous, some people find it very intrusive. Because we are bombarded with many messages in the course of a day, if we want to reconnect and not get lost in the shuffle, we need something that will stand out. Luckily, there is old-fashioned, tried and true method that works well in modern times.

One of the easiest ways to bridge the gap of time and overcome our own reluctance is to send a greeting card or a hand-written note. In this day of instant communication, people actually will appreciate your sending them something that is physical and cause them to stop and take notice.

Did you ever get something in the mail that was addressed by hand? Notice how the envelope stood out in the pile of bills, junk mail and other correspondence. Did it catch your eye so that it caused you to open it first? When you get a greeting card in the mail, it too stands out from the rest of the mail due to its shape and size. A greeting card with a simple message such as: "It's been a while since we were last in touch. I'd love to catch up with you" can motivate them to reach out to you.

> ***Instant Follow-Up in Just 1 Click[2]***
>
> *For a fast, simple way to send a real, personalized greeting card via first-class mail to someone in less than a minute and for under $2, I highly recommend using Sendoutcards. Try the system for free as my gift by going to sendoutcards.com/timhouston*

My friend, bestselling author and speaker Bob Burg believes in the hand-written note. For years, he uses a 8 by 3 ½ inch note card on which he sends a brief, hand-written note to the person he just met via first-class mail. As he says in his book, *Endless Referrals: Network Your Everyday Contacts into Sales*:

> *"The purpose of these note cards is not the sort of immediate results or instant-*

---

[2] Note: If you do become a client or a distributor for SendoutCards, I may be compensated by them in the form of a commission.

gratification ...nor is that what the process is designed to accomplish. It is designed to set the stage for future follow-up on your part."

Step 3: Design and Deliver the Message

Once you have done your homework and decided how the message is going to be delivered, it's time to craft the message. The message that you want to deliver needs to be designed for the recipient. Remember, your goal is to evoke a positive response: you want them to agree to communicate and/or meet with you.

You message could say something like:

"It's been a while since we were last in touch with each other and a lot has changed. Please call me so we can catch up."

"I came across your business card the other day and thought how long it's been since we heard from each other. I'd love to bring you up-to-date and I want to know how you are. Please call or email me this week so we can spend a few minutes catching up."

"They say that connections count more and more these days and we've been disconnected for a while. Can we reconnect so I can learn how I may be able to help you?"

"Congratulations! I heard that you recently (got married, had a child, got a promotion, adopted a puppy, etc.). I'd love to catch up with you. Please give me a call."

Step 4: Follow-Up!

Hopefully they have responded to your written request; however if after a few days you don't hear back from them, it is appropriate for you to give them a call to ensure that they received it. You could say something as simple as "Hi John, this is Jane Doe from XYZ Incorporated. I know we haven't talked in a while and I'm calling to find out if you got my recent note in the mail?"

In some cases, they may have moved and the mail wasn't forwarded. Maybe they got it but were distracted. Regardless of what they say, once you have made contact with your past referral partner, explain that because you enjoyed a good relationship in the past, (assuming it was a good one), you would like to reestablish contact. Remember, you are trying to help them to grow their business and you must have a genuine desire to help them. It's not about keeping score to see how many people they will refer to you at this given time.

Step 5: Set Up the Meeting

Ask to set up a meeting – no more than 1 hour in length – at their place of business or a neutral location such as a restaurant. A non-office location is preferred because it is free of workplace distractions. If you are in different cities and meeting in-person is a problem, use technology to your advantage through a scheduled video chat or, as a last resort, the good old-fashioned telephone call. Remember, your goal is not to sell them on your products or services but to get them to agree to meet or speak with you.

On the day of the meeting, keep the focus of the conversation on THEM, not you. Remember, you asked THEM to meet with you, so the conversation needs to be focused on how you can help them. You need to overcome their instinctual reaction of "what's in it for me."

Step 6: Ask Questions That Provide Value to Them

During your meeting, you could ask:

- "Could you provide me with an update about your products/services?"
- "What are some of the significant changes in your company or industry that occurred in the past year?"
- How is the economy is affecting your business?" (Don't be afraid to ask this

question because in tough economic times, people seem to expect you to ask it).

At some point in the conversation, you will ask how they get most of their business. They may say "advertising, cold-calls and mailings" Chances are, they will mention the words "referrals," "recommendations" or "word-of-mouth" somewhere in their answer;

Regardless of their answer ask this question:
"Are referrals helpful to your business?"

Then ask:
"What would an ideal referral be for you?"

If their answer is too general ("someone who needs our product/services"; "anyone in business" "everyone who is breathing" – you get the idea) your job is to help them to be specific. You can guide the conversation by asking the following:

"Joe, I'd like to help you to get those clients. It would help me if you could tell me where would I normally find such prospects?"

"Mary, I want to help you to refer those prospects to you. What should I listen for that would indicate this person needs your services?"

Bob, what should I say/ask/look for that would give me an indication that someone that needs your products or services? What should I say to them to make them receptive to having a conversation with you?"

The goal of your meeting is to show your referral partner that you care about THEIR success by asking them to teach you to spot referral opportunities. (You don't need to know the intricacies of their business; after all if you wanted to learn the "ins and outs" of their business, you'd be either working for them or competing against them).

As the potential referral giver, you want to know how your referral partner wants referrals to be delivered to them. Each of your referral partners will have different preferred methods. For example, if your referral source is a florist, she may say something like "just have them come to the shop and ask for me or my assistant, Maria and say that you referred them."

On the other hand, if your referral source is an accountant, he may say "Have them call or email my office to set up an appointment with me". Always find out your partner's preferred way of communicating (via phone, text, email, in-person, etc.).

Special Note: There are some professions whose conduct is dictated by a written code of ethics. You can still provide them with referrals but they must teach you how to do so within their ethical and legal boundaries. For example, if your friend was involved in a car accident and is in the hospital, an attorney who handles personal injury matters cannot go to a hospital to meet with an accident victim just because you told the attorney your friend was hurt. (That's what's commonly referred to as "ambulance chasing"). On the other hand, if your friend asked if you knew a good attorney he could consult with and asked for the attorney to call or for you to set up an appointment on his behalf, then falls within the attorney's ethical guidelines.

At the end of the meeting, pledge to refer someone to your referral partner in the near future. Make sure you agree upon on the definition of "near future" as every profession has a different time-frame. For a printer it could be within a few weeks; for a financial advisor, it could be several months.

Step 7: Touch Them Twice

After your leave the meeting, follow up with an email and a personal note or a greeting card. Be sure to thank your renewed referral partner for the time you spent together and reiterate your pledge to help them. The two-step process reinforces your commitment to your referral partner. While they may read the email today, they may "forget it" by the next week. But, they are reminded when they get the card or note.

Step 8: Make the Referral First

Whenever the opportunity presents itself, personally make the referral to your partner by contacting them in advance of the prospect's contact. If you are with the prospect, a technique I recommend is for you to call your referral partner so you can introduce them to each other and to allow them to set up a time to further communicate and/or meet. If you are not with the prospect, call your referral partner to alert them that the prospect will be contacting them, or better still, call your referral partner and give them the prospect's information so that they may follow-up. Be sure to secure the prospect's permission before having your referral partner communicate with them and advise your referral partner of the prospect's preferred method of communication.

From the point of view of both the prospect and the referral partner, you are "the connector" – the vital link – you are making it possible for these two people to communicate with each other. Not only does it help bridge the gap between the parties, but it positions you in both of their minds as someone who truly cares and who truly "walks the talk".

By reconnecting and building stronger bonds with those who are once again a part of our networks, we are working smarter instead of working harder. The end result will pay incredible dividends in our building our network, enhancing relationships and ultimately in our ability to give and receive referrals.

> *"Coming together is a beginning. Keeping together is progress. Working together is success."*
>
> *- Henry Ford*

RULE #6:

FOLLOW UP OR FALL OUT

The number one reason why most sales people fail at closing a sale or in getting existing customers to do business with them again and to refer new prospects is that they fail to follow up. For decades, there have been thousands of articles written and hundreds of studies conducted by university researchers and corporations that deal with the subject of follow up failure – from the initial inquiry to post sale.

It should be common sense then that one should follow up with the prospect almost immediately, and yet, there are many experienced people and long-time businesses that don't on a more routine basis than one would think. Some recent and notable studies about sales leads had some significant findings:

A March 2011 study published in the Harvard Business Review entitled "The Short Life of Online Sales Leads" revealed that 55% of companies do not respond at all to sales leads.

The Aberdeen Group and IDC released studies several years back showing that up to 70% of leads didn't get a follow up from sales if there wasn't a short term opportunity[vi].

Salesforce.com did a study of trade show exhibitors which found that 85% of the exhibitors did not follow up in any manner. Of the 15% that did follow up, 77% did within three weeks[vii].

Although the subject of this book is referrals and not sales leads, the impact of not following up on referrals can be disastrous not just for the individual receiving the referral and the image of their company, but for the referral source as well. Whenever someone gives you a referral, they have put their personal and professional reputation on the line as they usually have some sort of relationship with the prospect. They have entrusted the prospect to you and expect you to not only treat the prospect better than anyone else who comes by way of advertising and other marketing methods, they also expect you to make them – the source -- look good in the eyes of the prospect

How soon should you follow up after receiving a referral? If the referral came to you via one of your Referral Enablers or someone in one of your networks, you should first contact the source to clarify some information:

What is the relationship between the source and the prospect?

What did the prospect tell the source about their situation/challenge/issue/problem?

What did the source tell the prospect about you? If the source gave the prospect some inaccurate information, because they have the relationship with the prospect, they have an opportunity to go back to the prospect and clarify or correct it before you speak to the prospect. Not only does this enable them to save face it prevents embarrassment – theirs and yours.

Did the source tell the prospect when you should contact them and ask how they would prefer to be contacted? (Email? Text? Phone? In person?)

Depending on the nature of your business, would the prospect want the source to be present during your initial meeting or conversation?

After these questions are answered, then make the contact with the prospect. Once contact with the prospect is made, then follow up with the prospect. The more individualized and personalized the follow up, the more effective it will be. Don't just leave it to a telephone conversation or a one-time meeting.

Here are some effective follow-up methods – both time-tested and modern – that can work when following up with prospects:

Send them a card or a note of thanks. The power of a handwritten note has been proven over the ages to work very well. (Or as I mentioned earlier, SendoutCards will put a 21st Century twist is being able to send a physical card or note via the postal service through the internet for less than $2.00 – including postage).

If your prospect is on social media, get permission during your meeting to connect with them on Facebook, LinkedIn or Twitter or whatever social media outlets they participate in. Then reach out to thank them for meeting with you and follow-up by sharing articles, videos and other content that is appropriate. (Note: I don't mean inspirational memes on Instagram, chain-email/posts, and YouTube videos about cats, etc.) Give them something that's relevant and of value that you created, such as a blog post, a special report, or news article.

Film a short thank you video with your webcam or smartphone camera; upload it to YouTube as a private video. Then send an email note with the YouTube link so that they can watch it. Don't send the video as an email attachment as it may be too large and treated as spam or it may also be rejected by their email provider.

In your follow-up, always make it easy for them to contact you. Provide them with your email, your website, your phone number and (if appropriate), your social networking links. Don't assume that after you first meet or because the source gave your contact information that they will have it. It can be something as benign as a line as: "If I can be of any assistance or service to you, your family or friends, please contact me at…"

Whenever you get a referral your sources expect you to follow up with the prospect. Without follow-up you will fall out of favor and your referrals will be given to your competition. It shows your sources that you are worthy of their referrals; after all, they are giving you ***the privilege of the opportunity*** to potentially do business with someone who wants, needs or desires the products or services that you offer.

RULE #7:

GIVE THANKS...AND FEEDBACK

The vast majority of people learned at a very early age to say the magic words of "please" whenever they wanted something and "thank you" whenever they received something from someone. As adults sometimes we unintentionally forget even the most basic of manners. When one of our Referral Enablers or other sources gives a referral to us, there is an automatic tendency is to dive right into the sales process with the prospect to see if they really are qualified buy our services or products and if so, to make a sale.

Because time is of the essence, the very first thing we should whenever we get a referral do is to thank the Giver for providing us with the privilege of the opportunity. Make a phone call or send a quick email or a handwritten note to the person, showing your appreciation that they thought of you.

If the referral becomes a client, you may consider rewarding the referral source or you may want to just simply recognize them in a manner that they prefer. Dr. Ivan Misner, New York Times Bestselling Author and founder of BNI says: "[S]imple recognition really resonates with most people and, more often than not, simply recognizing people in the way they prefer to be recognized is a far better reward and incentive for them to refer you to others than offering them a cash finder's fee[viii]"

(In, *Leads to Referrals*, I provide several detailed, scalable methods and strategies on how to thank and reward the people who provide you with referrals, ranging from the simplest gestures to the most lavish of events).

But giving thanks is just one aspect of showing your gratitude, I believe it's also your responsibility to give feedback to the Giver of the referral as well as to get feedback from the Giver, regardless if the prospect became your client or not.

When you go back to the Giver to let them know:

- Did you reach the prospect or are you having difficulty doing so?
- Was the initial meeting arranged? Why/Why not?
- If the meeting took place, what was the outcome?
- If the person became your client, reinforce to the Giver why this was a great, qualified referral so that they could easily identify another who may be in similar circumstances or situations.

- If the person did not become your client or wasn't qualified, still thank the Giver but let them know what would be an ideal referral for you.

Ask the Giver to follow up with the prospect to find out how things went. Chances are that because of their relationship, the prospect will be more open and honest with the Giver than you. Then ask the Giver to give you clear, open and honest summary.

The old saying of "People don't care how much you know until they know how much you care" is so important to the referral generation process and is very noticeable. Feedback and saying thanks may seem like a small part of the referral generating process but it's these little things that can make a huge difference in your business.

BEFORE YOU GO...

I want to thank you for reading ***The Referral Rules.*** If you found the book to be enjoyable, useful, educational or helpful in anyway, I would be very grateful if you would post a short review on Amazon.com or your country's amazon site.

I believe that anyone who is a teacher must also be an eternal student as well. Your feedback is greatly appreciated and helps me to continuously improve in order to deliver a quality experience for you, the reader.

To leave a review, all you need to do is go to the following link on Amazon:
http://amzn.to/1gyCT9E

Remember to check out the official Facebook page where you can share your success stories, tips and strategies for generating referrals with other business people from around the world. Just go to **www.facebook.com/referralrules** and like the page.

    If I can be of service to you, your company or organization – ranging from keynote speaking and training to customized workshops and trainings, please contact me at **www.tmhouston.com**

Follow me on Twitter: **@tmhouston**

Follow me on Periscope: **www.periscope.tv/timhouston**

MEET TIM HOUSTON

The super-simple bio: He's a father, a #1 Bestselling Author, in-demand Speaker, a high-energy motivational Trainer and an Entrepreneur with 20+ years of making businesses and people more productive, profitable and prosperous.

The "Official Bio": Tim Houston is an entrepreneur who has started, owned and/or managed four businesses during the past 20 years. Still a small business owner, his advice and authority is from continuous, daily experience "in the trenches — not from the ivory tower."

He the author of three #1, international bestselling books: (*The World's Worst Networker*, *Leads to Referrals* and *The Referral Rules!*) and a contributor to the New York Times, and #1 Wall Street Journal and USA Today bestseller, **Masters of Sales**.

Whether as an in-demand keynote speaker, a high-energy trainer or through his online programs, he has worked with business people in more than 60 countries to become more productive, profitable and prosperous.

IN HIS OWN WORDS:

"I like to think of myself as a guy who, after 20 years of real-life business experience, often offers unique and sometimes common-sense approaches to solving what seems like complex problems for businesspeople."

"I have been very fortunate to work with people from around the world who come from all walks of life and are at different levels of success. I love teaching them how to make their networking and referral marketing and generation efforts to be more productive, profitable and prosperous."

ENDNOTES

[i] dictionary.reference.com/browse/privilege

[ii] www.thefreedictionary.com/enabler.

[iii] Influencer Guidebook 2013. Published by the Word of Mouth Marketing Association. 2013

[iv] Vossoughi, S. (2008 April 11) "It's All About The Experience." www.businessweek.com/stories/2008-04-11/its-all-about-experiencebusinessweek-business-news-stock-market-and-financial-advice

[v] Pine II, Joseph B. and James H. Gillmore. *The Experience Economy,* Updated Edition, page 5, Harvard Business Review Press; Updated edition (July 5, 2011)

[vi] Vanella, M. *Nine Ways To Get Your Salespeople To Follow Up On More Leads*, CSO Insights & The Vanella Forum. Retrieved from http://www.vanellagroup.com/documents/2013Nine_Ways_to_Sales_Rep_Lead_Followup_VanellaGroup.pdf

[vii] Source: **www.salesforcetraining.com/sales-training-blog/sales-management-training/are-your-salespeople-squandering-tradeshow-leads/**. (Accessed 18th September 2013).

[viii] Source: **businessnetworking.com/simple-recognition-is-sometimes-the-best-reward**. (Accessed 24th September 2013)

www.ingramcontent.com/pod-product-compliance
Lightning Source LLC
Chambersburg PA
CBHW021017180526
45163CB00005B/1989